THE GOSPEL
OF WEALTH

The Condensed Classics Library

THE GOSPEL
OF WEALTH

The Definitive Edition of the
Wealth-Building Classic

Andrew Carnegie

Expanded and Introduced
by Mitch Horowitz

THE CONDENSED CLASSICS LIBRARY™

Published by Gildan Media LLC
aka G&D Media.
www.GandDmedia.com

The Gospel of Wealth was originally published in 1889
The Best Fields for Philanthropy was originally published 1889
The Gospel of Wealth II was originally published in 1906

G&D Media Condensed Classics edition published 2021

Introduction copyright © 2021 by Mitch Horowitz

FIRST PRINT AND EBOOK EDITION: 2021

Cover design by David Rheinhardt of Pyrographx

Interior design by Meghan Day Healey of Story Horse, LLC.

ISBN: 978-1-7225-0078-8

CONTENTS

The Gospel of Carnegie

By Mitch Horowitz

Success author Napoleon Hill described his first encounter with steel magnate Andrew Carnegie—"the richest man that the richest nation on earth ever produced"—in terms that brought to mind Moses receiving the tablets on Mount Sinai. Hill said that he interviewed the industrialist in 1908 and received marching orders to codify a philosophy of success, which formed the basis for his 1928 book *The Law of Success* and the wealth-building classic that followed nine years later, *Think and Grow Rich*.

Whatever impression Hill left on Carnegie, the industrialist made no mention of the younger man in his writings. Nor did Hill begin making references to the fateful meeting until nearly a decade after Carnegie's death in 1919. Critics question whether the encounter ever took place. I am agnostic on the point. Hill was working that year for *Bob Taylor's Magazine*, an inspirational and general-interest monthly that featured up-by-the-bootstraps stories of millionaires—a staple of the day's popular literature—and the job could have facilitated contact between journalist and subject. In any case, Carnegie's memoirs do paint the image of a man who enjoyed discussing the metaphysics of success. In his autobiography, published posthumously in 1920, Carnegie recalled that as an adolescent he "became deeply interested in the mysterious doctrines of Swedenborg." A Spiritualist aunt encouraged the young Carnegie to develop his psychical talents, or "ability to expound 'spiritual sense.'"

Carnegie was eager to be taken seriously as an author and he reveled in probing whether there exist natural laws of money and accumulation. In June 1889, Carnegie published his essay "Wealth" for the *North American Review,* which might have been forgotten if not for its near-immediate republication by England's evening newspaper *The Pall Mall Gazette* under the more alluring title by which it became internationally famous and is reprinted here: "The Gospel of Wealth."

Taking a leaf from the neo-Darwinian views of philosopher Herbert Spencer, Carnegie described a "law of competition," which he believed brought a rough, necessary order to the world:

> *While the law may be sometimes hard to the individual, it is best for the race, because it ensures the survival of the fittest in every department. We accept and welcome, therefore, as conditions to which we must accommodate ourselves, great inequality of environment, the concentration of business, industrial and commercial, in the hands of a few, and the law of competition between these, as being not only beneficial but essential for the future progress of the race.*

Although contemporaneous success authors such as Ralph Waldo Trine and Wallace D. Wattles extolled creativity above competition, Carnegie welcomed "laws of accumulation" as a necessary means of separating life's winners from losers. At his steel mills, the magnate sometimes backed his belief through ruthless and, by way of surrogates and business partners, brutal labor practices. Seven of his workers were killed by Pinkerton guards during the Homestead Strike of 1892.

Yet Carnegie's essay had a surprising wrinkle. He emphasized that great wealth—which he attributed chiefly to raw materials, real estate, utilities, and inventions (the manufacturer disdained financial speculation)—was the product of the community. And should ultimately be returned to it. Wealth, Carnegie argued, is amassed as a passive result of an industrialist or investor benefiting from mass shifts in demography, migration, and public needs. The world's reputedly richest man wrote that wealth should be restored to the community rather than passed down through family inheritance. In a sentiment that would win him few admirers among radicals and reformers, Carnegie counseled that millionaires should electively dispense their money in acts of philanthropy during their lifetimes. He called that the legitimate culmination of success. In essence, Carnegie argued that monopolistic capitalism should be leavened by voluntary largesse or noblesse oblige. But the millionaire's sense of volunteerism had its limits. If the rich didn't find a way to disperse their fortunes through philanthropy, Carnegie called for a nearly 100 percent estate tax to settle the matter for them.

"The Gospel of Wealth" proved so popular that Carnegie issued two sequels in the *North American Review*— the first in December 1889 called "The Best Fields for Philanthropy" and the second seventeen years later in December 1906 called "The Gospel of Wealth II."

In this Condensed Classics edition I have combined all three "Gospel" essays for a panoramic view of Carnegie's wealth philosophy. I have excised, shortened, or clarified a few policy references or news-related tangents reflective of his immediate era, and also eliminated some superfluous prefatory material so that these three works can be read as one whole. I have modernized spellings and added a few clarifying footnotes. Although Carnegie wrote a handful of related pieces in response to his critics, these interwoven essays provide a more or less complete perspective on his views of how wealth is generated—and how it should be dispensed.

Whether one agrees with Carnegie on every point—and I do not—it is worth noting that he followed through on his statements with wide-ranging acts of structured philanthropy. In so doing, the industrialist helped presage the nonprofit field as it exists today. His business advice is for each individual to assess, but of one point he leaves no doubt: great fortunes accrue due not primarily to the ability of their holders but to ancillary events and circumstances that emerge from public need and growth.

The Gospel of Wealth

The problem of our age is the proper administration of wealth, so that the ties of brotherhood may still bind together the rich and poor in harmonious relationship. The conditions of human life have not only been changed, but revolutionized, within the past few hundred years. In former days there was little difference between the dwelling, dress, food, and environment of the chief and those of his retainers. The Indians are today where civilized man then was. When visiting the Sioux, I was led to the wigwam of the chief. It was just like the others in external appearance, and even within the difference was trifling between it and those of the poorest of his braves. The contrast between the palace of the millionaire and the cottage of the laborer with us today measures the change which has come with civilization.

This change, however, is not to be deplored, but welcomed as highly beneficial. It is well, nay, essential for the progress of the race, that the houses of some should be homes for all that is highest and best in literature and the arts, and for all the refinements of civilization, rather than that none should be so. Much better this great irregularity than universal squalor. Without wealth there can be no Mæcenas.* The "good old times" were not good old times. Neither master nor servant was as well situated then as today. A relapse to old conditions would be disastrous to both—not the least so to him who serves—and would sweep away civilization with it. But whether the change be for good or ill, it is upon us, beyond our power to alter, and therefore to be accepted and made the best of. It is a waste of time to criticize the inevitable.

It is easy to see how the change has come. One illustration will serve for almost every phase of the cause. In the manufacture of products we have the whole story. It applies to all combinations of human industry, as stimulated and enlarged by the inventions of this scientific age. Formerly articles were manufactured at the domestic hearth or in small shops which formed part of the

---

* Carnegie refers here to the wealthy Roman statesman who was a patron to the arts.

household. The master and his apprentices worked side by side, the latter living with the master, and therefore subject to the same conditions. When these apprentices rose to be masters, there was little or no change in their mode of life, and they, in turn, educated in the same routine succeeding apprentices. There was, substantially, social equality, and even political equality, for those engaged in industrial pursuits had then little or no political voice in the State.

But the inevitable result of such a mode of manufacture was crude articles at high prices. Today the world obtains commodities of excellent quality at prices which even the generation preceding this would have deemed incredible. In the commercial world similar causes have produced similar results, and the race is benefited thereby. The poor enjoy what the rich could not before afford. What were the luxuries have become the necessaries of life. The laborer has now more comforts than the landlord had a few generations ago. The farmer has more luxuries than the landlord had, and is more richly clad and better housed. The landlord has books and pictures rarer, and appointments more artistic, than the King could then obtain.

The price we pay for this salutary change is, no doubt, great. We assemble thousands of operatives in the factory, in the mine, and in the counting-house, of whom the employer can know little or nothing, and to whom the employer is little better than a myth. All intercourse between them is at an end. Rigid Castes are formed, and, as usual, mutual ignorance breeds mutual distrust. Each Caste is without sympathy for the other, and ready to credit anything disparaging in regard to it. Under the law of competition, the employer of thousands is forced into the strictest economies, among which the rates paid to labor figure prominently, and often there is friction between the employer and the employed, between capital and labor, between rich and poor. Human society loses homogeneity.

The price which society pays for the law of competition, like the price it pays for cheap comforts and luxuries, is also great; but the advantages of this law are also greater still, for it is to this law that we owe our wonderful material development, which brings improved conditions in its train. But, whether the law be benign or not, we must say of it, as we say of the change in the conditions of men to which we have referred: It is here; we cannot evade it; no substitutes for it have been found; and while the law may be sometimes hard for the individual, it is best for the race, because it ensures the survival of the fittest in every department. We accept and welcome therefore, as conditions to which we must accommodate ourselves, great inequality of environment, the concentration of business, industrial and commercial, in the hands of a few, and the law of competition between these, as being not only beneficial, but essential for the future progress of the race. Having accepted these, it follows that there must be great scope for the exercise of special ability in the merchant and in the manufacturer who has to conduct affairs upon a great scale. That this talent for organization and management is rare among men is proved by the fact that it invariably secures for its possessor enormous rewards, no matter where or under what laws or conditions. The experienced in affairs always rate the MAN whose services can be obtained as a partner as not only the first consideration, but such as to render the question of his capital scarcely worth considering, for such men soon create capital; while, without the special talent required, capital soon takes wings. Such men become interested in firms or corporations using millions; and estimating only simple interest to be made upon the capital invested, it is inevitable that their income must exceed their expenditures, and that they must accumulate wealth. Nor is there any middle ground which such men can occupy, because the great manufacturing or commercial concern which does not earn at least interest upon its capital soon becomes bankrupt. It must either go forward or fall behind: to stand still is impossible. It is a condition essential for its successful operation that it should be thus far profitable, and even that, in addition to interest on capital, it should make profit. It is a law, as certain as any of the others named, that men possessed of this peculiar talent for affair, under the free play of economic forces, must, of necessity, soon be in receipt of more revenue than can be judiciously expended upon themselves; and this law is as beneficial for the race as the others.

Objections to the foundations upon which society is based are not in order, because the condition of the race is better with these than it has been with any others which have been tried. Of the effect of any new substitutes proposed we cannot be sure. The Socialist or Anarchist who seeks to overturn present conditions is to be regarded as attacking the foundation upon which civilization itself rests, for civilization took its start from the day that the capable, industrious workman said to his incompetent and lazy fellow, "If thou dost not sow, thou shalt not reap," and thus ended primitive Communism by separating the drones from the bees. One who studies this subject will soon be brought face to face with the conclusion that upon the sacredness of property civilization itself depends—the right of the laborer to his hundred dollars in the savings bank, and equally the legal right of the millionaire to his millions.

To these who propose to substitute Communism for
this intense Individualism the answer, therefore, is: The
race has tried that. All progress from that barbarous
day to the present time has resulted from its displace-
ment. Not evil, but good, has come to the race from the
accumulation of wealth by those who have the ability
and energy that produce it. But even if we admit for
a moment that it might be better for the race to dis-
card its present foundation, Individualism—that it is
a nobler ideal that man should labor, not for himself
alone, but in and for a brotherhood of his fellows, and
share with them all in common, realizing Swedenborg's
idea of Heaven, where, as he says, the angels derive
their happiness, not from laboring for self, but for each
other—even admit all this, and a sufficient answer is,
This is not evolution, but revolution. It necessitates the
changing of human nature itself a work of aeons, even
if it were good to change it, which we cannot know.
It is not practicable in our day or in our age. Even if
desirable theoretically, it belongs to another and long-
succeeding sociological stratum. Our duty is with what
is practicable now; with the next step possible in our
day and generation. It is criminal to waste our energies
in endeavoring to uproot, when all we can profitably
or possibly accomplish is to bend the universal tree of
humanity a little in the direction most favorable to the

production of good fruit under existing circumstances. We might as well urge the destruction of the highest existing type of man because he failed to reach our ideal as favor the destruction of Individualism, Private Property, the Law of Accumulation of Wealth, and the Law of Competition; for these are the highest results of human experience, the soil in which society so far has produced the best fruit. Unequally or unjustly, perhaps, as these laws sometimes operate, and imperfect as they appear to the Idealist, they are, nevertheless, like the highest type of man, the best and most valuable of all that humanity has yet accomplished.

We start, then, with a condition of affairs under which the best interests of the race are promoted, but which inevitably gives wealth to the few. Thus far, accepting conditions as they exist, the situation can be surveyed and pronounced good. The question then arises—and, if the foregoing be correct, it is the only question with which we have to deal—What is the proper mode of administering wealth after the laws upon which civilization is founded have thrown it into the hands of the few? And it is of this great question that I believe I offer the true solution. It will be understood that *fortunes* are here spoken of, not moderate sums saved by many years of effort, the returns on which are required for the comfortable maintenance and educa-

tion of families. This is not *wealth,* but only *competence*
which it should be the aim of all to acquire.

There are but three modes in which surplus wealth
can be disposed of. It can be left to the families of the
decedents; or it can be bequeathed for public purposes;
or, finally, it can be administered during their lives by
its possessors. Under the first and second modes most
of the wealth of the world that has reached the few has
hitherto been applied. Let us in turn consider each
of these modes. The first is the most injudicious. In
monarchical countries, the estates and the greatest portion of the wealth are left to the first son, that the vanity
of the parent may be gratified by the thought that his
name and title are to descend to succeeding generations
unimpaired. The condition of this class in Europe today
teaches the futility of such hopes or ambitions. The successors have become impoverished through their follies
or from the fall in the value of land. Even in Great Britain the strict law of entail has been found inadequate
to maintain the status of an hereditary class. Its soil is
rapidly passing into the hands of the stranger. Under
republican institutions the division of property among
the children is much fairer, but the question which
forces itself upon thoughtful men in all lands is: Why
should men leave great fortunes to their children? If this
is done from affection, is it not misguided affection?

Observation teaches that, generally speaking, it is not well for the children that they should be so burdened. Neither is it well for the state. Beyond providing for the wife and daughters moderate sources of income, and very moderate allowances indeed, if any, for the sons, men may well hesitate, for it is no longer questionable that great sums bequeathed oftener work more for the injury than for the good of the recipients. Wise men will soon conclude that, for the best interests of the members of their families and of the state, such bequests are an improper use of their means.

It is not suggested that men who have failed to educate their sons to earn a livelihood shall cast them adrift in poverty. If any man has seen fit to rear his sons with a view to their living idle lives, or, what is highly commendable, has instilled in them the sentiment that they are in a position to labor for public ends without reference to pecuniary considerations, then, of course, the duty of the parent is to see that such are provided for *in moderation*. There are instances of millionaires' sons unspoiled by wealth, who, being rich, still perform great services in the community. Such are the very salt of the earth, as valuable as, unfortunately, they are rare; still it is not the exception, but the rule, that men must regard, and, looking at the usual result of enormous sums conferred upon legatees, the thoughtful man must shortly say, "I would as soon leave to my son a curse as the almighty dollar," and admit to himself that it is not the welfare of the children, but family pride, which inspires these enormous legacies.

As to the second mode, that of leaving wealth at death for public uses, it may be said that this is only a means for the disposal of wealth, provided a man is content to wait until he is dead before it becomes of much good in the world. Knowledge of the results of legacies bequeathed is not calculated to inspire the brightest hopes of much posthumous good being accomplished. The cases are not few in which the real object sought by the testator is not attained, nor are they few in which his real wishes are thwarted. In many cases the bequests are so used as to become only monuments of his folly. It is well to remember that it requires the exercise of not less ability than that which acquired the wealth to use it so as to be really beneficial to the community. Besides this, it may fairly be said that no man is to be extolled for doing what he cannot help doing, nor is he to be thanked by the community to which he only leaves wealth at death. Men who leave vast sums in this way may fairly be thought men who would not have left it at all, had they been able to take it with them. The memories of such cannot be held in grateful remembrance, for there is no grace in their gifts. It is not to be wondered at that such bequests seem so generally to lack the blessing.

The growing disposition to tax more and more heavily large estates left at death is a cheering indication of the growth of a salutary change in public opinion. The State of Pennsylvania now takes—subject to some exceptions—one-tenth of the property left by its citizens. The budget presented in the British Parliament the other day proposes to increase the death-duties; and, most significant of all, the new tax is to be a graduated one. Of all forms of taxation, this seems the wisest. Men who continue hoarding great sums all their lives, the proper use of which for public ends would work good to the community, should be made to feel that the community, in the form of the state, cannot thus be deprived of its proper share. By taxing estates heavily at death the state marks its condemnation of the selfish millionaire's unworthy life.

It is desirable that nations should go much further in this direction. Indeed, it is difficult to set bounds to the share of a rich man's estate which should go at his death to the public through the agency of the state, and by all means such taxes should be graduated, beginning at nothing upon moderate sums to dependents, and increasing rapidly as the amounts swell, until of the millionaire's hoard, as of Shylock's, at least—The other half Comes to the privy coffer of the state.

This policy would work powerfully to induce the rich man to attend to the administration of wealth during his life, which is the end that society should always have in view, as being that by far most fruitful for the people. Nor need it be feared that this policy would sap the root of enterprise and render men less anxious to accumulate, for to the class whose ambition it is to leave great fortunes and be talked about after their death, it will attract even more attention, and, indeed, be a somewhat nobler ambition to have enormous sums paid over to the state from their fortunes.

There remains, then, only one mode of using great fortunes; but in this we have the true antidote for the temporary unequal distribution of wealth, the reconciliation of the rich and the poor—a reign of harmony—another ideal, differing, indeed, from that of the Communist in requiring only the further evolution of existing conditions, not the total overthrow of our civilization. It is founded upon the present most intense individualism, and the race is projected to put it in practice by degree whenever it pleases. Under its sway we shall have an ideal state, in which the surplus wealth of the few will become, in the best sense the property of the many, because administered for the common good, and this wealth, passing through the hands of the few, can be made a much more potent force for the elevation of our race than if it had been distributed in small sums to the people themselves. Even the poorest can be made to see this, and to agree that great sums gathered by some of their fellow-citizens and spent for public purposes, from which the masses reap the principal benefit, are more valuable to them than if scattered among them through the course of many years in trifling amounts.

If we consider what results flow from the Cooper Institute, for instance, to the best portion of the race in New York not possessed of means, and compare these with those which would have arisen for the good of the masses from an equal sum distributed by Mr. Cooper in his lifetime in the form of wages, which is the highest form of distribution, being for work done and not for charity, we can form some estimate of the possibilities for the improvement of the race which lie embedded in the present law of the accumulation of wealth. Much of this sum if distributed in small quantities among the people, would have been wasted in the indulgence of appetite, some of it in excess, and it may be doubted whether even the part put to the best use, that of adding to the comforts of the home, would have yielded results for the race, as a race, at all comparable to those which are flowing and are to flow from the Cooper Institute from generation to generation. Let the advocate of violent or radical change ponder well this thought.

We might even go so far as to take another instance, that of Mr. Tilden's bequest of five millions of dollars for a free library in the city of New York, but in referring to this one cannot help saying involuntarily, how much better if Mr. Tilden had devoted the last years of his own life to the proper administration of this immense sum; in which case neither legal contest nor any other cause of delay could have interfered with his aims.* But let us assume that Mr. Tilden's millions finally become the means of giving to this city a noble public library, where the treasures of the world contained in books will be open to all forever, without money and without price. Considering the good of that part of the race which congregates in and around Manhattan Island, would its permanent benefit have been better promoted had these millions been allowed to circulate in small sums through the hands of the masses? Even the most strenuous advocate of Communism must entertain a doubt upon this subject. Most of those who think will probably entertain no doubt whatever.

Poor and restricted are our opportunities in this life; narrow our horizon; our best work most imperfect;

---

* Carnegie refers here to the bequest of wealthy American statesman Samuel J. Tilden, which was subject to numerous legal challenges by his family after Tilden's death in 1886.

but rich men should be thankful for one inestimable boon. They have it in their power during their lives to busy themselves in organizing benefactions from which the masses of their fellows will derive lasting advantage, and thus dignify their own lives. The highest life is probably to be reached, not by such imitation of the life of Christ as Count Tolstoi gives us, but, while animated by Christ's spirit, by recognizing the changed conditions of this age, and adopting modes of expressing this spirit suitable to the changed conditions under which we live; still laboring for the good of our fellows, which was the essence of his life and teaching, but laboring in a different manner.

This, then, is held to be the duty of the man of Wealth: First, to set an example of modest, unostentatious living, shunning display or extravagance; to provide moderately for the legitimate wants of those dependent upon him; and after doing so to consider all surplus revenues which come to him simply as trust funds, which he is called upon to administer, and strictly bound as a matter of duty to administer in the manner which, in his judgment, is best calculated to produce the most beneficial results for the community—the man of wealth thus becoming the mere agent and trustee for his poorer brethren, bringing to their service his superior wisdom, experience and ability to administer, doing for them better than they would or could do for themselves.

We are met here with the difficulty of determining what are moderate sums to leave to members of the family; what is modest, unostentatious living; what is the test of extravagance. There must be different standards for different conditions. The answer is that it is as impossible to name exact amounts or actions as it is to define good manners, good taste, or the rules of propriety; but, nevertheless, these are verities, well known although undefinable. Public sentiment is quick to know and to feel what offends these. So in the case of wealth. The rule in regard to good taste in the dress of men or women applies here. Whatever makes one conspicuous offends the canon. If any family be chiefly known for display, for extravagance in home, table, equipage, for enormous sums ostentatiously spent in any form upon itself, if these be its chief distinctions, we have no difficulty in estimating its nature or culture. So likewise in regard to the use or abuse of its surplus wealth, or to generous, freehanded cooperation in good public uses, or to unabated efforts to accumulate and hoard to the last, whether they administer or bequeath. The verdict rests with the best and most enlightened public sentiment. The community will surely judge and its judgments will not often be wrong.

The best uses to which surplus wealth can be put have already been indicated. These who would administer wisely must, indeed, be wise, for one of the serious obstacles to the improvement of our race is indiscriminate charity. It were better for mankind that the millions of the rich were thrown into the sea than so spent as to encourage the slothful, the drunken, the unworthy. Of every thousand dollars spent in so-called charity today, it is probable that $950 is unwisely spent; so spent, indeed as to produce the very evils which it proposes to mitigate or cure. A well-known writer of philosophic books admitted the other day that he had given a quarter of a dollar to a man who approached him as he was coming to visit the house of his friend. He knew nothing of the habits of this beggar; knew not the use that would be made of this money, although he had every reason to suspect that it would be spent improperly. This man professed to be a disciple of Herbert Spencer; yet the quarter-dollar given that night will probably work more injury than all the money which its thoughtless donor will ever be able to give in true charity will do good. He only gratified his own feelings, saved himself from annoyance—and this was probably one of the most selfish and very worst actions of his life, for in all respects he is most worthy.

In bestowing charity, the main consideration should be to help those who will help themselves; to provide part of the means by which those who desire to improve may do so; to give those who desire to use the aids by which they may rise; to assist, but rarely or never to do all. Neither the individual nor the race is improved by almsgiving. Those worthy of assistance, except in rare cases, seldom require assistance. The really valuable men of the race never do, except in cases of accident or sudden change. Everyone has, of course, cases of individuals brought to his own knowledge where temporary assistance can do genuine good, and these he will not overlook. But the amount which can be wisely given by the individual for individuals is necessarily limited by his lack of knowledge of the circumstances connected with each. He is the only true reformer who is as careful and as anxious not to aid the unworthy as he is to aid the worthy, and, perhaps, even more so, for in almsgiving more injury is probably done by rewarding vice than by relieving virtue.

The rich man is thus almost restricted to following the examples of Peter Cooper, Enoch Pratt of Baltimore, Mr. Pratt of Brooklyn, Senator Stanford, and others, who know that the best means of benefiting the community is to place within its reach the ladders upon which the aspiring can rise—parks, and means of recreation, by which men are helped in body and mind; works of art, certain to give pleasure and improve the public taste, and public institutions of various kinds, which will improve the general condition of the people—in this manner returning their surplus wealth to the mass of their fellows in the forms best calculated to do them lasting good.

Thus is the problem of Rich and Poor to be solved. The laws of accumulation will be left free; the laws of distribution free. Individualism will continue, but the millionaire will be but a trustee for the poor; entrusted for a season with a great part of the increased wealth of the community, but administering it for the community far better than it could or would have done for itself. The best minds will thus have reached a stage in the development of the race in which it is clearly seen that there is no mode of disposing of surplus wealth creditable to thoughtful and earnest men into whose hands it flows save by using it year by year for the general good. This day already dawns. Man may die without incurring the pity of their fellows, still sharers in great business enterprises from which their capital cannot be or has not been withdrawn, and is left chiefly at death for public uses, yet the man who dies leaving behind many millions of available wealth, which was his to administer during life, will pass away "unwept, unhonored, and unsung," no matter to what uses he leaves the dross which he cannot take with him. Of such as these the public verdict will then be: "The man who dies thus rich dies disgraced."

Such, in my opinion, is the true Gospel concerning Wealth, obedience to which is destined someday to solve the problem of the Rich and the Poor, and to bring "Peace on earth, among men Good-Will."

Some argue that the gospel of wealth is not lived up to by the acts. To this the reply seems obvious: the gospel of Christianity is also killed by the acts. The same objection that is urged against the gospel of wealth lies against the commandment "Thou shalt not steal." It is no argument against a gospel that it is not lived up to; indeed, it is an argument in its favor, for a gospel must be higher than the prevailing standard. It is no argument against a law that it is broken: in that disobedience lies the reason for making and maintaining the law; the law which is never to be broken is never required.

Let us turn attention to some of the best methods of performing this duty of administering surplus wealth for the good of the people. The first requisite for a really good use of wealth by the millionaire who has accepted the gospel which proclaims him only a trustee of the surplus that comes to him is to take care that the purpose for which he spends it shall not have a degrading, pauperizing tendency upon its recipients, and that his trust should be so administered as to stimulate the best and most aspiring poor of the community to further efforts for their own improvement. It is not the irreclaimably destitute, shiftless, and worthless that it is truly beneficial or truly benevolent to attempt to reach and improve. For these there exists the refuge provided by the city or the state, where they can be sheltered, fed, clothed, and kept in comfortable existence, and—most important of all—where they can be isolated from the well-doing and industrious poor, who are liable to be demoralized by contact with these unfortunates. One man or woman who succeeds in living comfortably by begging is more dangerous to society, and a greater obstacle to the progress of humanity, than a score of wordy Socialists. The individual administrator of surplus wealth has as his charge the industrious and ambitious; not those who need everything done for them, but those who, being most anxious and able to help themselves, deserve and will be benefited by help from others and the extension of their opportunities at the hands of the philanthropic rich.

It is ever to be remembered that one of the chief obstacles which the philanthropist meets in his efforts to do real and permanent good in this world is the practice of indiscriminate giving; and the duty of the millionaire is to resolve to cease giving to objects that are not proved clearly to his satisfaction to be deserving. He must remember Mr. Rice's belief, that nine hundred and fifty out of every thousand dollars bestowed today upon so-called charity had better be thrown into the sea. As far as my experience of the wealthy extends, it is unnecessary to urge them to give of their superabundance in charity so-called. Greater good for the race is to be achieved by inducing them to cease impulsive and injurious giving. As a rule, the sins of millionaires in this respect are not those of omission, but of commission, because they will not take time to think, and chiefly because it is much easier to give than to refuse. Those who have surplus wealth give millions every year which produce more evil than good, and which really retard the progress of the people, because most of the forms in vogue today for benefiting mankind only tend to spread among the poor a spirit of dependence upon alms, when what is essential for progress is that they should be inspired to depend upon their own exertions. The miser millionaire who hoards his wealth does less injury to society than the careless millionaire who squanders his unwisely, even if he does so under cover of the mantle of sacred charity. The man who gives to the individual beggar commits a grave offense, but there are many societies and institutions soliciting alms which it is nonetheless injurious to the community to aid. These are as corrupting as individual beggars. Plutarch's "Morals" contains this lesson: "A beggar asking an alms of a Lacedaemonian, he said: 'Well, should I give thee anything, thou wilt be the greater beggar, for he that first gave thee money made thee idle, and is the cause of this base and dishonorable way of living'." As I know them, there are few millionaires, very few indeed, who are clear of this sin of having made beggars.

Bearing in mind these considerations, let us endeavor to present some of the best uses to which a millionaire can devote the surplus of which he should regard himself as only the trustee.

First—Standing apart by itself there is the founding of a university by men enormously rich, such men as must necessarily be few in any country. Perhaps the greatest sum ever given by an individual for any purpose is the gift of Senator Stanford, who undertakes to establish upon the Pacific coast, where he amassed his enormous fortune, a complete university, which is said to involve the expenditure of ten millions of dollars, and upon which he may be expected to bestow twenty millions of his surplus. He is to be envied. A thousand years hence some orator, speaking his praise upon the then-crowded shores of the Pacific, may repeat Griffith's eulogy of Wolsey, "In bestowing he was most princely: ever witness for him this great seat of learning." Here is a noble use of wealth.

We have many such institutions, Hopkins, Cornell, Packer, and others, but most of these have only been bequeathed, and it is impossible to extol any man greatly for simply leaving what he cannot take with him. Cooper, and Pratt, and Stanford, and others of this class deserve credit and the admiration of their fellows as much for the time and the attention given during their lives, as for their expenditure, upon their respective monuments.

We cannot have the Pacific coast in mind without recalling another important work of a different character which has recently been established there, the Lick Observatory. If any millionaire be interested in the ennobling study of astronomy—and there should be and would be such if they but gave the subject the slightest attention—here is an example which could well be followed, for the progress made in astronomical instruments and appliances is so great and continuous that every few years a new telescope might be judiciously given to one of the observatories upon this continent, the last being always the largest and the best, and cer-

tain to carry further and further the knowledge of the
universe and of our relation to it here upon the earth.
As one among many of the good deeds of the late Mr.
Thaw, of Pittsburg, his constant support of the observatory there may be mentioned. This observatory enabled
Professor Langley to make his wonderful discoveries.
The professor is now at the head of the Smithsonian
Institution, a worthy successor to Professor Henry.
Connected with him was Mr. Braeshier, of Pittsburg,
whose instruments are in most of the principal observatories of the world. He was a common millwright,
but Mr. Thaw recognized his genius and was his main
support through trying days. This common workman
has been made a professor by one of the foremost scientific bodies of the world. In applying part of his surplus
in aiding these two now famous men, the millionaire
Thaw did a noble work. Their joint labors have brought
great, and are destined to bring still greater, credit upon
their country in every scientific center throughout the
world.

It is reserved for very few to found universities,
and, indeed, the use for many, or perhaps any, new
universities does not exist. More good is henceforth to
be accomplished by adding to and extending those in
existence. But in this department a wide field remains
for the millionaire as distinguished from the Croesus

among millionaires.* The gifts to Yale University have been many, but there is plenty of room for others. The School of Fine Arts, founded by Mr. Street, the Sheffield Scientific School, endowed by Mr. Sheffield, and Professor Loomis's fund for the observatory, are fine examples. Mrs. O.J. Osborne's building for reading and recitation is to be regarded with especial pleasure as being the wise gift of a woman. Harvard University has not been forgotten; the Peabody Museum, and the halls of Wells, Matthews, and Thayer may be cited. Seber Hall is worthy of special mention, as showing what a genius like Richardson could do with the small sum of a hundred thousand dollars. The Vanderbilt University at Nashville, Tennessee, may be mentioned as a true product of the gospel of wealth. It was established by members of the Vanderbilt family during their lives— mark this vital feature—during their lives; for nothing counts for much that is left by a man at his death. Such funds are torn from him, not given by him. If any millionaire is at a loss to know how to accomplish great and indisputable good with his surplus, here is a field which can never be fully occupied, for the wants of our universities increase with the development of the country.

---

* Carnegie refers to the ancient Greek ruler who conquered parts of Persia and was legendary for his wealth.

Second—The result of my own study of the question, What is the best gift which can be given to a community? is that a free library occupies the first place, provided the community will accept and maintain it as a public institution, as much a part of the city property as its public schools, and, indeed, an adjunct to these. It is, no doubt, possible that my own personal experience may have led me to value a free library beyond all other forms of beneficence. When I was a boy in Pittsburg, Colonel Anderson, of Allegheny—a name I can never speak without feelings of devotional gratitude—opened his little library of four hundred books to boys. Every Saturday afternoon he was in attendance himself at his house to exchange books. No one but he who has felt it can know the intense longing with which the arrival of Saturday was awaited, that a new book might be had. My brother and Mr. Phipps, who have been my principal business partners through life, shared with me Colonel Anderson's precious generosity, and it was when reveling in these treasures that I resolved, if ever wealth came to me, that it should be used to establish free libraries, that other poor boys might receive opportunities similar to those for which we were indebted to that noble man.

Great Britain has been foremost in appreciating the value of free libraries for its people. Parliament passed an act permitting towns and cities to establish and maintain these as municipal institutions, and whenever the people of any town or city voted to accept the provisions of the act, the authorities were authorized to tax the community to the extent of one penny in the pound valuation. Most of the towns already have free libraries under this act. Many of these are the gifts of rich men, whose funds have been used for the building, and in some cases for the books also, the communities being required to maintain and to develop the libraries; and to this feature I attribute most of their usefulness. An endowed institution is liable to become the prey of a clique. The public ceases to take interest in it, or, rather, never acquires interest in it. The rule has been violated which requires the recipients to help themselves. Everything has been done for the community instead of its being only helped to help itself.

Many free libraries have been established in our country, but none that I know of with such wisdom as the Pratt Library, of Baltimore. Mr. Pratt presented to the city of Baltimore one million dollars, requiring it to pay 5 percent, per annum, amounting to fifty thousand dollars per year, which is to be devoted to the maintenance and development of the library and its branches. During last year 430,217 books were distributed; 37,196 people of Baltimore are registered upon the books as readers; and it is safe to say that the 37,000 frequenters of the Pratt Library are of more value to Baltimore, to the State, and to the country than all the inert, lazy, and hopelessly-poor in the whole nation. And it may further be safely said that, by placing within the reach of 37,000 aspiring people books which they were anxious to obtain, Mr. Pratt has done more for the genuine progress of the people than has been done by all the contributions of all the millionaires and rich people to help those who cannot help themselves. The one wise administrator of his surplus has poured his fertilizing stream upon soil that was ready to receive it and return a hundred-fold. The many squanderers have not only poured their streams into sieves which never can be filled—they have done worse; they have poured them into stagnant sewers that breed the diseases which afflict the body politic. And this is not all. The million dollars of which Mr. Pratt has made so grand a use are something, but there is something greater still. When the fifth branch library was opened in Baltimore, the speaker said:

> *Whatever may have been done in these four years, it was his pleasure to acknowledge that much, very much, was due to the earnest interest, the wise councils, and the practical suggestions*

of Mr. Pratt. He never seemed to feel that the mere donation of great wealth for the benefit of his fellow-citizens was all that would be asked of him, but he wisely labored to make its application as comprehensive and effective as possible. Thus he constantly lightened burdens that were, at times, very heavy, brought good cheer and bright sunshine when clouds flitted across the sky, and made every officer and employee feel that good work was appreciated, and loyal devotion to duty would receive hearty commendation.

This is the finest picture I have ever seen of any of the millionaire class. As here depicted, Mr. Pratt is the ideal disciple of the "Gospel of Wealth." We need have no fear that the mass of toilers will fail to recognize in such as he their best leaders and their most invaluable allies; for the problem of poverty and wealth, of employer and employed, will be practically solved whenever the time of the few is given, and their wealth is administered during their lives, for the best good of that portion of the community which has not been burdened by the responsibilities which attend the possession of wealth. We shall have no antagonism between classes when that day comes, for the high and the low, the rich and the poor, shall then indeed be brothers.

No millionaire will go far wrong in his search for one of the best forms for the use of his surplus who chooses to establish a free library in any community that is willing to maintain and develop it. John Bright's words should ring in his ear: "It is impossible for any man to bestow a greater benefit upon a young man than to give him access to books in a free library." Closely allied to the library, and, where possible, attached to it, there should be rooms for an art gallery and museum, and a hall for such lectures and instruction as are provided in the Cooper Union. The traveler upon the Continent is surprised to find that every town of importance has its art gallery and museum; these may be large or small, but in any case each has a receptacle for the treasures of the locality, which is constantly receiving valuable gifts and bequests. The free library and art gallery of Birmingham are remarkable among these, and every now and then a rich man adds to their value by presenting books, fine pictures, or other works of art. All that our cities require to begin with is a proper fireproof building. Their citizens who travel will send to it rare and costly things from every quarter of the globe they visit, while those who remain at home will give or bequeath to it of their treasures. In this way these collections will grow until our cities will ultimately be able to boast of permanent exhibitions from which their own citizens will derive incalculable benefit, and which they will be proud to show to visitors. In the Metropolitan Museum of Art in this city we have made an excellent beginning. Here is another avenue for the proper use of surplus wealth.

Third—We have another most important department in which great sums can be worthily used—the founding or extension of hospitals, medical colleges, laboratories, and other institutions connected with the alleviation of human suffering, and especially with the prevention rather than the cure of human ills. There is no danger of pauperizing a community in giving for such purposes, because such institutions relieve temporary ailments or shelter only those who are hopeless invalids. What better gift than a hospital can be given to a community that is without one ?—the gift being conditioned upon its proper maintenance by the community in its corporate capacity. If hospital accommodation already exists, no better method for using surplus wealth can be found than in making additions to it. The late Mr. Vanderbilt's gift of half a million of dollars to the medical department of Columbia College for a chemical laboratory was one of the wisest possible uses of wealth. It strikes at the prevention of disease by penetrating into its causes. Several others have established such laboratories, but the need for them is still great.

If there be a millionaire in the land who is at a loss what to do with the surplus that has been committed to him as trustee, let him investigate the good that is flowing from these chemical laboratories. No medical college is complete without its laboratory. As with universities, so with medical colleges; it is not new institutions that are required, but additional means for the more thorough equipment of those that exist. The forms that benefactions to these may wisely take are numerous, but probably none is more useful than that adopted by Mr. Osborne when he built a school for training female nurses at Bellevue College. If from all gifts there flows one-half of the good that comes from this wise use of a millionaire's surplus, the most exacting may well be satisfied. Only those who have passed through a lingering and dangerous illness can rate at their true value the care, skill, and attendance of trained female nurses. Their employment as nurses has enlarged the sphere and influence of woman. It is not to be wondered at that a Senator of the United States and a physician distinguished in this country for having received the highest distinctions abroad should find their wives from this class.

Fourth—In the very front rank of benefactions public parks should be placed, always provided that the community undertakes to maintain, beautify, and preserve inviolate the parks given to it. No more useful or more beautiful monument can be left by any man than a park for the city in which he was born or in which he has long lived, nor can the community pay a more graceful tribute to the citizen who presents it than to give his name to the gift. If a park be already provided, there is still room for many judicious gifts in connection with it. Mr. Phipps, of Allegheny, has given conservatories to the park there, which are visited by many every day of the week and crowded by thousands of working people every Sunday, for, with rare wisdom, he has stipulated as a condition of the gift that the conservatories shall be open on Sundays. The result of his experiment has been so gratifying that he is justified in adding to them from his surplus, as he is doing largely this year. To any lover of flowers among the wealthy I commend a study of what is possible for them to do in the line of Mr. Phipps's example; and may they please note that Mr. Phipps is a wise as well as a liberal giver, for he requires the city to maintain these conservatories, and thus secures for them forever the public ownership, the public interest, and the public criticism of their management. Had he undertaken to manage and maintain them, it is probable that popular interest in the gift would never have been awakened.

The parks and pleasure-grounds of small towns throughout Europe are not less surprising than their libraries, museums, and art galleries. We saw nothing more pleasing during our recent travels than the hillside of Bergen, in Norway. It has been converted into one of the most picturesque of pleasure-grounds; fountains, cascades, waterfalls, delightful arbors, fine terraces, and statues adorn what was before a barren mountainside. Here is a field worthy of study by the millionaire who would confer a lasting benefit upon his fellows. Another beautiful instance of the right use of wealth in the direction of making cities more and more attractive we found in Dresden. The owner of the leading paper there bequeathed its revenues forever to the city, to be used in beautifying it. An art committee decides from time to time what new artistic feature is to be introduced or what hideous feature is to be changed, and as the revenues accrue they are expended in this direction. Thus through the gift of this patriotic newspaper proprietor his native city of Dresden is fast becoming one of the most artistic places of residence in the whole world.

A work having been completed, it devolves upon the city to maintain it forever. May I be excused if I commend to our millionaire newspaper proprietors the example of their colleague in the capital of Saxony?

Scarcely a city of any magnitude in the older countries is without many structures and features of great beauty. Much has been spent upon ornament, decoration, and architectural effect: we are still far behind in these things upon this side of the Atlantic. Our Republic is great in some things—in material development unrivalled; but let us always remember that in art and in the finer touches we have scarcely yet taken a place. Had the exquisite memorial arch recently erected temporarily in New York been shown in Dresden, the art committee there would probably have been enabled, from the revenue of the newspaper given by its owner for just such purposes, to order its permanent erection to adorn the city forever.

While the bestowal of a park upon a community as one of the best uses for surplus wealth will be universally approved, in embracing such additions to it as conservatories, or in advocating the building of memorial arches and works of adornment, it is probable that many will think we go too far, and consider these somewhat fanciful. The material good to flow from them may not be so directly visible; but let not any practical mind, intent only upon material good, depreciate the value of wealth given for these or for kindred aesthetic purposes as being useless as far as the mass of the people and their needs are concerned. As with libraries and museums, so with these more distinctively artistic works; these perform their great use when they reach the best of the masses of the people. It is worth more to reach and touch the sentiment for beauty in the naturally bright minds of this class than that those incapable of being so touched should be pandered to. For what the improver of the race must endeavor to do is to reach those who have the divine spark ever so feebly developed, that it may be strengthened and grow. For my part, I think Mr. Phipps put his money to better use in giving the workingmen of Allegheny conservatories filled with beautiful flowers, orchids, and aquatic plants, which they, with their wives and children, can enjoy in their spare hours, and on which they can feed the love for the beautiful, than if he had given his surplus money to furnish them with bread, for those in health who cannot earn their bread are scarcely worth considering by the individual giver; the care of such being the duty of the state. The man who erects in a city a truly artistic arch, statue, or fountain makes a wise use of his surplus. "Man does not live by bread alone."

Fifth—We have another good use for surplus wealth, in providing for our cities halls suitable for meetings of all kinds, especially for concerts of elevating music. Our cities are rarely provided with halls for these purposes, being in this respect also very far behind European cities. The Springer Hall, of Cincinnati, that valuable addition to the city, was largely the gift of Mr. Springer, who was not content to bequeath funds from

his estate at death, but who gave during his life, and,
in addition, gave—what was equally important—his
time and business ability to ensure the successful results
which have been achieved. The gift of a hall to any city
lacking one is an excellent use for surplus wealth for the
good of a community. The reason why the people have
only one instructive and elevating, or even amusing,
entertainment when a dozen would be highly beneficial, is that the rent of a hall, even when a suitable hall
exists (which is rare), is so great as to prevent managers
from running the risk of financial failure. If every city
in our land owned a hall which could be given or rented
for a small sum for such gatherings as a committee or
the mayor of the city judged advantageous, the people
could be furnished with proper lectures, amusements,
and concerts at an exceedingly small cost. The town
halls of European cities, many of which have organs,
are of inestimable value to the people, when utilized as
they are in the manner suggested. Let no one underrate
the influence of entertainments of an elevating or even
of an amusing character, for these do much to make the
lives of the people happier and their natures better. If
any millionaire born in a small village, which has now
become a great city, is prompted in the day of his success to do something for his birthplace with part of his
surplus, his grateful remembrance cannot take a form

more useful than that of a public hall with an organ, provided the city agrees to maintain and use it.

Sixth—In another respect we are still much behind Europe. A form of beneficence which is not uncommon there is providing swimming baths for the people. The donors of these have been wise enough to require the city benefited to maintain them at its own expense, and as proof of the contention that everything should never be done for anyone or for any community, but that the recipients should invariably be called upon to do part, it is significant that it is found essential for the popular success of these healthful establishments to exact a nominal charge for their use. In many cities, however, the school children are admitted free at fixed hours upon certain days, different hours being fixed for the boys and the girls to use the great swimming baths, hours or days being also fixed for the use of these baths by ladies. In inland cities the young of both sexes are thus taught to swim. Swimming clubs are organized, and matches are frequent, at which medals and prizes are given. The reports published by the various swimming baths throughout Great Britain are filled with instances of lives saved because those who fortunately escaped shipwreck had been taught to swim in the baths, and not a few instances are given in which the pupils of certain bathing establishments have saved the lives of others. If any disciple of the "Gospel of Wealth "gives his favorite city large swimming and private baths (provided the municipality undertakes their management as a city affair), he will never be called to account for an improper use of the funds entrusted to him.

Seventh—Churches as fields for the use of surplus wealth have purposely been reserved until the last, because, these being sectarian, every man will be governed by his own attachments; therefore gifts to churches, it may be said, are not, in one sense, gifts to the community at large, but to special classes. Nevertheless, every millionaire may know of a district where the little cheap, uncomfortable, and altogether unworthy wooden structure stands at the crossroads, to which the whole neighborhood gathers on Sunday, and which is the center of social life and source of neighborly feeling. The administrator of wealth has made a good use of part of his surplus if he replaces that building with a permanent structure of brick, stone, or granite, up the sides of which the honeysuckle and columbine may climb, and from whose tower the sweet-tolling bell may sound. The millionaire should not figure how cheaply this structure can be built, but how perfect it can be made. If he has the money, it should be made a gem, for the educating influence of a pure and noble specimen of architecture, built, as the pyramids were built, to stand for ages, is not to be measured by dollars. Every farmer's home, heart, and mind in the district will be influenced by the beauty and grandeur of the church. But having given the building, the donor should stop there; the support of the church should be upon its own people; there is not much genuine religion in the congregation or much good to flow from the church which is not supported at home.

Many other avenues for the wise expenditure of surplus wealth might be indicated. I enumerate but a few—a very few—of the many fields which are open, and only those in which great or considerable sums can be judiciously used. It is not the privilege, however, of millionaires alone to work for or aid measures which are certain to benefit the community. Every one who has but a small surplus above his moderate wants may share this privilege with his richer brothers, and those without surplus can give at least part of their time, which is usually as important as funds, and often more so. Someday, perhaps, with your permission, I will endeavor to point out some fields and modes in which these may perform well their part as trustees of wealth or leisure, according to the measure of their respective fortunes.

It is not expected, neither is it desirable, that there should be a general concurrence as to the best possible use of surplus wealth. For different men and different

localities there are different uses. What commends itself
most highly to the judgment of the administrator is the
best use for him, for his heart should be in the work. It
is as important in administering wealth as it is in any
other branch of a man's work that he should be enthu-
siastically devoted to it and feel that in the field selected
his work lies. Besides this, there is room and need for all
kinds of wise benefactions for the common weal. The
man who builds a university, library, or laboratory per-
forms no more useful work than he who elects to devote
himself and his surplus means to the adornment of a
park, the gathering together of a collection of pictures
for the public, or the building of a memorial arch. These
are all true laborers in the vineyard. The only point
required by the "Gospel of Wealth" is that the surplus
which accrues from time to time in the hands of a man
should be administered by him in his own lifetime for
that purpose which is seen by him, as trustee, to be best
for the good of the people. To leave at death what he
cannot take away, and place upon others the burden of
the work which it was his own duty to perform, is to
do nothing worthy. This requires no sacrifice, nor any
sense of duty to his fellows.

Time was when the words concerning the rich man
entering heaven were regarded as a hard saying. Today,
when all questions are probed to the bottom and the

standards of faith receive the most liberal interpretations, the startling verse has been relegated to the rear, to await the next kindly revision as one of those things which cannot be quite understood, but which meanwhile—it is carefully to be observed—are not to be understood literally. But is it so very improbable that the next stage of thought is not to restore the doctrine in all its pristine purity and force, as being in perfect harmony with sound ideas upon the subject of wealth and poverty, the rich and the poor, and the contrasts everywhere seen and deplored? In Christ's day, it is evident, reformers were against the wealthy. It is nonetheless evident that we are fast recurring to that position today; and there will be nothing to surprise the student of sociological development if society should soon approve the text which has caused so much anxiety: "It is easier for a camel to enter the eye of a needle than for a rich man to enter the Kingdom of Heaven." Even if the needle were the small casement at the gates, the words betoken serious difficulty for the rich. It will be but a step for the theologian to take from the doctrine that he who dies rich dies disgraced to that which brings upon the man punishment or deprivation hereafter.

The "Gospel of Wealth" but echoes Christ's words. It calls upon the millionaire to sell all that he hath and give it in the highest and best form to the poor, by administering his estate himself for the good of his fellows, before he is called upon to lie down and rest upon the bosom of Mother Earth. So doing, he will approach his end no longer the ignoble hoarder of useless millions, poor, very poor indeed, in money, but rich, very rich, twenty times a millionaire still, in the affection, gratitude, and admiration of his fellow-men, and—sweeter far—soothed and sustained by the still small voice within, which, whispering, tells him that, because he has lived, perhaps one small part of the great world has been bettered just a little. This much is sure: against such riches as these no bar will be found at the Gates of Paradise.

The problem of wealth will not down. It is obviously so unequally distributed that the attention of civilized man must be attracted to it from time to time. He will ultimately enact the laws needed to produce a more equal distribution. It is again foremost in the public mind today.

We have evidence of this in President Teddy Roosevelt's recent speech of April 14th, 1906, in which he gives direct and forcible expression to public sentiment. We quote:

> *It is important to this people to grapple with the problems connected with the amassing of enor-*

mous fortunes, and the use of those fortunes, both corporate and individual, in business. We should discriminate in the sharpest way between fortunes well won and fortunes ill won; between those gained as an incident to performing great services to the community as a whole, and those gained in evil fashion by keeping just within the limits of mere law-honesty. Of course, no amount of charity in spending such fortunes in any way compensates for misconduct in making them. As a matter of personal conviction, and without pretending to discuss the details or formulate the system, I feel that we shall ultimately have to consider the adoption of some such scheme as that of a progressive tax on all fortunes beyond a certain amount, either given in life or devised or bequeathed upon death to any individual—a tax so framed as to put it out of the power of the owner of one of these enormous fortunes to hand on more than a certain amount to any one individual; the tax, of course, to be imposed by the national and not the State government. Such taxation should, of course, be aimed merely at the inheritance or transmission in their entirety of those fortunes swollen beyond all healthy limits.

It is seventeen years since *The North American Review* published "The Gospel of Wealth," written by this writer, which strongly urged graduated taxation of estates at death of possessors as the easiest and best mode of ensuring for the community a just share of great fortunes. He is in full accord with the President's views, as quoted, upon this vital question. Continued study has only confirmed him in his conviction of their justice, their beneficent effect upon society, and their necessity in the not-distant future. Much has been written of a contrary character. Graduated taxation has been denounced as unjust and Socialistic, fatal to Individualism and sure to sap the springs of enterprise. If the writer thought it favorable to Socialism or Communism, or in the least degree opposed to Individualism, he would be the last to favor it, for of nothing is he more fully convinced than that in Individualism lies the secret of the steady progress of civilization. Except we build upon the foundation of "As ye sow so shall ye reap," we labor in vain to establish a higher, or even to maintain the present, civilization. Virtue must bring reward, vice punishment, work wages, sloth misery. Energy and skill must win a prize denied to indolence and ignorance. He who sows the wind must reap the whirlwind.

The rights of private property emerged slowly from ages when property was held mostly in common; as civilization advanced men became less communistic and more individualistic. Public sentiment at last sustained private property because it was found favorable, and discarded Communism because it was found unfavorable, to progress; but there is nothing sacred about individual ownership except as man has established it as the system under which progress can be made. There is no cause to fear, therefore, that man is ever to turn round and creep backward toward the barbarism from which he has finally emerged. The law of evolution forbids, for his march is upward. Should he go too far in assessing wealth, he will inevitably reverse his action and adopt that policy which is best for the general good.

First, as to the justice of taxing large fortunes left at death upon a graduated scale for the benefit of the community. Graduated taxes are no new feature. Britain long since adopted them.

They are advocated by no less an authority than Adam Smith, who says, "The subjects of every state ought to contribute to the support of government as nearly as possible in proportion to their respective abilities."

Let us go to the root of the matter and inquire how these fortunes are created, from whence and how they arise.

Imagine an honest hardworking farmer who finds himself able to give to each of his two sons a farm. They have married admirable young women of the neighborhood, of good kith and kin, friends from youth—no mistake about their virtues. The sons find farms, one in the center of Manhattan Island, the other beyond the Harlem. They cast lots for the farms as the fairest method, thus letting the fates decide. Neither has a preference. The Harlem farm falls to the elder, the Manhattan to the younger. Mark now the problem of wealth, how it develops.

A few hundred dollars buy the farms, and the loving brothers set out for themselves. They are respected by all; loved by their intimates. To the extent of their means, they are liberal contributors to all good causes, and especially to the relief of neighbors who through exceptional troubles need friendly aid and counsel. They are equally industrious, cultivate their farms equally well and in every respect are equally good citizens of the state. Their children grow up and are educated together.

The growth of New York City northwards soon makes the children of the younger millionaires, while those of the elder remain simple farmers in comfortable circumstances, but still of the class who, fortunate in this beyond their cousins, have to perform some service to their fellows and thus earn a livelihood.

Now, who or what made this difference in wealth? Not labor, not skill. No, nor superior ability, sagacity, nor enterprise, nor greater public service. The Community created the millionaire's wealth. While he slept, it grew as fast as when he was awake. It would have arisen exactly as it did had he been on the Harlem and his brother on the Manhattan farm.

The younger farmer, now a great property-holder, dies and his children in due time pass away, each leaving millions, since the farm has become part of a great city, and immense buildings upon it produce annual rents of hundreds of thousands of dollars.

When these children die, who have neither toiled nor spun, what canon of justice would be violated were the nation to step in and say that, since the aggregation of their fellow men called "the community" created the decedent's wealth, it is entitled to a large portion of it as they pass away. The community has refrained from exacting any part during their lives. The heirs have been allowed to enjoy it all, because although in their case the wealth was a purely communal growth, yet in other cases wealth often comes largely from individual effort and ability, and hence it is better for the community to allow such ability to remain in charge of fortune-making, because most likely to succeed, and in so doing develop our country's resources.

It would be unwise to interfere with the working bees; better allow them to continue gathering honey during their lives. When they die, the nation should have a large portion of the honey remaining in the hives; it is immaterial at what date collection is made, so that it comes to the National Treasury at last.

In a prosperous country, increasing rapidly in population, like our own, by far the greatest amount of wealth created in any department comes from enhanced values of real property.

The census shows that from 1890 to 1900 the value of real estate increased by nearly $13 billion.

The obvious creator of this wealth is not the individual but the community, as we see in the case of the two brother farmers. Property may pass through many proprietors, each paying more for it than his predecessor; but whether each succeeding owner sells to his successor at a profit depends almost solely upon whether the surrounding population increases. Let population remain stationary and so do values of property. Let it decline, and values fall even more rapidly. In other words, increased population—the community—creates the wealth in each successive generation. Decrease of population reduces it, and this law holds in the whole of that vast and greatest field of wealth, real estate. In no other field is the making of wealth so greatly dependent upon the community, so little upon the owner, who may wholly neglect it without injury. Therefore no other form of wealth should contribute to the nation so generously.

Let us now trace the acquisition of wealth by the active businessman who has some personal part, and often not a small one, in creating it.

Imagine four brothers, sons of another hardworking farmer. The first settles in New York City, the second in Pittsburgh, the third in Chicago and the fourth in Montana. The first sees that railroads in every direction are essential to the coming Metropolis and devotes himself to this field, obtains large interests therein; and, as the population of the country increases and that of New York City bounds ahead into the millions, these lines of transport laden with traffic justify increasing bonded debt. Having the figures under his eye, he sees that the shares of these railways are sure to become dividend-paying, that even already there are surplus earnings beyond the bonded interest, which, if not needed for pressing extensions, could be paid in dividends and make the stock par. He strains his credit, borrows great sums, buys the shares when prices are low, and, floating upon a tidal wave of swelling prosperity, caused by the increased traffic of rapidly increasing communities, he soon becomes a multimillionaire and at his death his children are all left millionaires. In the consolidation of the various short lines into one great whole there was margin for a stupendous increase of capital; and in other collateral fields there lay numerous opportunities for profitable exploitation, all, however, dependent upon an expanding population for increased values. Now, while the founder of the family must be credited with remarkable ability and with having done the state some service in his day and generation, it cannot be denied that the chief creator of his wealth was the increasing communities along the railroads, which gave the traffic that lifted these lines into dividend-payers upon a capital far beyond the actual cost of the property.

In the work and its profits the nation was an essential partner, and equally entitled with the individual to share in the dividends.

The second son is so fortunate as to settle in Pittsburgh when it has just been discovered that some of the coalfields of which it is the center produced a coking-coal admirably adapted for iron-ore smelting. Another vein easily mined proved a splendid steam-coal. Small iron mills soon sprang up. Everything indicated that here was indeed the future iron city, where steel could be produced more cheaply than in any other location in the world. Naturally, his attention was turned in this direction. He wooed the genius of the place. This was not anything extraordinarily clever. It was in the air. He is entitled to credit for having abiding faith in the future of his country and of steel, and for risking with his young companions not only all he had, which was little or nothing, but all they could induce timid bankers to lend from time to time. He and his partners built mills and furnaces, and finally owned a large concern making millions yearly. This son and his partners looked ahead. They visited other lands and noted conditions, and finally concluded that a large supply of raw materials was the key to permanent prosperity. Accordingly, they bought or leased many mines of iron ore, many thousands of acres of coal and of limestone and also of natural-gas territory, and at last had for many long years a full supply of all the minerals required to produce iron and steel. This was wise policy, but it did not require genius, only intelligent study and good judgment, to see that. They did not produce these minerals; they saw them lying around open for sale at prices that are now deemed only nominal. Much of the wealth of the concern came from these minerals which were once the public property of the community, and were easily secured by this fortunate son and his partners upon trifling royalties.

Their venture was made profitable by the demand for their products, iron and steel, from the expanding population engaged in settling a new continent. Without new populous communities far and near, no milliondom was possible for them. The increasing population was always the important factor in their success. Why should the Nation be denied participation in the results when the gatherers cease to gather and a division has to be made?

The third son was attracted to Chicago, and quite naturally became an employee in a meatpacking concern, in which he soon made himself indispensable. A small interest in the business was finally won by him, and he rose in due time to millionairedom, just as the population of the country swelled. If Chicago today, and our country generally, had only the population of early days, there could have been no great fortune for the third son. Here, as before, it was the magnitude of the business, based solely upon the wants of the population, that swelled the yearly profits and produced prodigious fortunes.

The fourth son, attracted by the stories of Hecla and Calumet, and other rich mines which "far surpass the wealth of Ormus or of Ind" settled in Montana and was lucky after some years of rude experience. His ventures gave him the coveted millionairedom. The amount of copper and silver required by the teeming population of the country and of other lands kept prices high, and hence his enormous profits mined from land for which only a trifle was paid to the General Government not so long ago. He did not create his wealth; he only dug it out of the mine as the demands of the people gave value to the previously worthless stones. Here especially we cannot but feel that the people who created the value should share the dividends when these must pass into other hands.

The fifth son had a melancholy career. He settled in New York City while young and unfortunately began his labors in a stockbroker's office, where he soon became absorbed in the fluctuations of the Exchange, while his fond mother proudly announced to all she met that he "was in business." From this the step was easy to taking chances with his small earnings.

His gambling ventures proved successful. It was an era of rising values, and he soon acquired wealth without increasing values, for speculation is the parasite of business feeding upon values, creating none. A few years and the feverish life of the gamester told upon him. He was led into a scheme to corner a certain stock, and, as was to have been expected, he found that men who will conspire to entrap others will not hesitate to deceive their partners upon occasion if sure it will pay and be safe from exposure. He ended his life by his own hand. His end serves to keep his brothers resolute in the resolve never to gamble. The speculator seldom leaves a millionaire's fortune, unless he breaks down or passes away when his ventures are momentarily successful. In such a case, his ill-gotten gold should be levied upon by the state at the highest rate of all, even beyond that imposed upon real estate values. Wealth is often, we may say generally, accumulated in such manner as benefits the nation in the process; here the means employed demoralizes the getter as well as the people, and lowers the standard of ethics. It is taken without returning any valid consideration.

There is one class of millionaires whose wealth in very much greater degree than others may be credited to themselves. Graham Bell of the telephone, Edison of numerous inventions, Westinghouse of the airbrake, and others, who originated or first applied processes hitherto unused, and were sufficiently alive to their pecuniary interests to hold large shares in the companies formed to develop and introduce them to the public. Their wealth had its origin in their own inventive brains. All honor to the inventor! He stands upon a higher platform than the others.

It may be said that in greater or less degree our leading manufacturers, railroad-builders, department-store projectors, meatpackers, and other specialists in one line or other had to adopt new methods; and, with few, if any, exceptions, there can be traced in their careers some special form of ability upon which their success depended, thus distinguishing them from the mass of competitors. No doubt this is correct, yet the inventions or processes used were the work of others, so that all they did was to introduce new methods of management or to recognize and utilize opportunities. This the inventor class have also done if they have become millionaires, but in addition they have invented the new processes. So that these deserve to reap beyond the other class, yet only in degree, because both classes alike depend upon increasing population—the masses, who require, or consume, the article produced, so that even the inventor's wealth is in great part dependent upon the community which uses his productions.

It is difficult to understand why, at the death of its possessor, great wealth, gathered or created in any of these or in other forms, should not be shared by the community which has been the most potent cause or partner of all in its creation. We have seen that enormous fortunes are dependent upon the community; without great and increasing population, there could be no great wealth. Where wealth accrues honorably, the people are always silent partners.

It is not denied that the great administrator, whether as railroad-builder, steamship-owner, manufacturer, merchant, banker, is an exceptional man, or that millions honestly made in any useful occupation give evidence of ability, foresight, and assiduity above the common and prove the man who has made them a valuable member of society. In no wise, therefore, should such men be unduly hampered or restricted as long as they are spared. After all, they can absorb comparatively little; and, generally speaking, the money-making man, in contrast to his heirs, who generally become members of the smart or fast set, is abstemious, retiring and little of a spendthrift. The millionaire himself is probably the least expensive bee in the industrial hive, taking into account the amount of honey he gathers and what he consumes.

An Income Tax is sometimes proposed as one of the best possible modes of correcting the uneven distribution of wealth, but of all taxes this is the most pernicious. It demoralizes a nation. Mr. Gladstone, one of the greatest financial ministers, advocated its abolition in Britain, alleging that it made a "Nation of Liars." During the Civil War, we had such a tax and paid it loyally, but public sentiment demanded its repeal and it was the first tax remitted when war ceased—justly so because it penalized the honest citizen. Its imposition would be strenuously opposed unless it were graduated and the exemption line placed high, so that the tax should be restricted to the few enormous fortunes. The Supreme Court has declared such a tax to be unconstitutional. No great gain would result to the state from it compared to what would accrue from the easier plan of exacting heavy taxes at death. The date of collection matters little, so that the payment is certain at last. Such proportions can be exacted as are deemed proper from time to time, until it is generally agreed that great wealth at last pays its fair share to the people of the Nation, who were so highly instrumental in creating it or from whom it was gathered.

The collection of an Income Tax would require a large trained body of permanent officials to collect from indignant, discontented people, naturally resenting intrusive inquiries regarding their private affairs. The honest would always pay, the dishonest would usually escape. Much better that Corporations should be required to pay a dividend tax to the Nation which would be really a tax upon Incomes. It is by doing so that Britain realizes such enormous sums from its Income Tax. Were she to attempt to collect these direct from each individual, it would be found much less productive. So should we find if we made the attempt. There is no reason for so doing. Every dividend-paying Corporation can be made the rigid collector of Income Tax for the Government.

It is clearly at the rich man's death that the community should exact a large share of estate, a graduated share, increasing in proportion to its extent. It should be paid over to the Government and applied to the service of the people, the silent but contributive partner from whom it has been so largely derived. The graduated death duties exacted by Britain might guide us in the beginning. The maximum assessment upon estates to the lineal successors is eight percent, upon the valuation, but to distant legatees it is very much higher. Smaller estates pay less in proportion.

Such contributions from the owners of enormous fortunes at death would do much to reconcile dissatisfied but fair-minded people to the alarmingly unequal distribution of wealth arising from the new industrial conditions of our day and the era of unprecedented prosperity our country has enjoyed for years.

The millionaire himself should rejoice at the thought of being a useful laborer in the national vineyard and in knowing that his contribution to the general fund at death will lessen the drain upon the scanty resources of his less successful fellows. Wealth left at death seldom does better service than this.

The people see how equivocally in many cases, how unfairly in others, fortunes have been made. Especially have the numerous failures of prominent men in official position to perform their duties properly deeply impressed them, and produced a strong feeling of antagonism to wealth and millionaires as a class. The appeal to them in the June number of this *Review* should not pass unheeded. As wealth comes mainly from the community, it should be administered as a sacred trust, by the temporary recipient, for the public good. Property in one sense is a mere creature of the law. Whether the holder be permitted to bequeath it to his successors and to what extent and how, are simply questions of policy for the people through the Government to determine. France has long restricted it. Our States generally designate the widow's share. There is here no question of right or wrong, but simply one of policy—what is best in all respects for the Nation.

Fortunes have recently been more easily made with us than ever, both in number and amount, with the inevitable result that sudden wealth is bound to produce in a new land, which, not so long ago, was much freer from immense fortunes than the older lands of Europe. Millionaires are a recent growth in the Republic. Multimillionaires were unheard of before our day.

Some sixty-odd years ago, Britain, then in the beginning of the speculative period of railroad construction and manufacturing supremacy, had a somewhat similar experience. Greater fortunes were made than ever before; but the makers, imbued with the aristocratic ambition to become great landowners and county magnates, were soon absorbed into that class. They regarded wealth only as a means to an end—entrance to the aristocratic and fashionable circle. This refuge new millionaires lack under our democratic system, hence the vulgar, extravagant and offensive character of the follies to which they are driven, that evoke so much adverse criticism from people of education, good sense, and quiet respectable living, with whom mere dollars count for little. Funds collected by the Government from the estates of the millionaires at death would never be likely otherwise to be put to so good a use as the payment of Government expenditures, relieving the people in part from the burden of taxation.

We are yet as a nation in the heyday of youth. In time we shall tone down and live simpler lives and create different standards. Wealth will be dethroned as higher tastes prevail, its pursuit become less absorbing and less esteemed, and, above all, the mere man of wealth himself will come to realize that in the estimation of those of wisest judgment he has no place with the educated, professional man. He occupies a distinctly lower plane intellectually, and in the coming day Brain is to stand above Dollars, Conduct above both. The making of money as an aim will then be rated as an ignoble ambition. No man has ever secured recognition, much less fame, from mere wealth. It confers no distinction among the good or the great.

Meanwhile, as the masses become more intelligent, they may be expected to criticize and denounce the growth of fortunes which fail to contribute largely to the public good, and finally to insist that they shall be made to do so. The first step to this end should be heavy graduated death taxes upon wealth, in pursuance of Adam Smith's dictum already quoted.

Indications of alarm are sometimes seen regarding present conditions. Fears are expressed that a war of classes may arise. On the contrary, there are none but healthful signs in the awakening intelligence and deep interest of the masses in this problem. Its final solution upon right lines cannot but place the body politic in a much better position than before.

The American people can be trusted to deal with improper methods of business and excessive wealth accumulations wisely and well, to the advantage of the Nation, as they have met and solved other pressing problems, some of which for a time were thought by many likely to cause serious trouble, whereas the commotion only indicated that another step nearer the light was about to be taken. So will it be with this new problem of regulating, as needed, both corporations and individuals, that there may be fairer acquisition and fairer distribution of wealth.

About the Authors

Born in Scotland in 1835, Andrew Carnegie migrated with his parents to the United States in 1848 at age twelve. The family settled in Allegheny, Pennsylvania, where Andrew took his first job at age 13 at the local cotton mill. After a series of jobs and ventures, Carnegie became a steel manufacturer in Pittsburgh where he grew wealthy through supplying steel during the nation's industrial boom. By 1901, he sold Carnegie Steel to JP Morgan making Carnegie arguably the richest man in the world. The industrialist spent the remaining two decades of life writing and organizing his fortune into philanthropic trusts. He died in Lennox, Massachusetts, in 1919.

Mitch Horowitz is the PEN Award-winning author of books including *Occult America* and *The Miracle Club*. Mitch introduces and edits G&D Media's line of Condensed Classics and is the author of the Napoleon Hill Success Course series including *The Miracle of a Definite Chief Aim* and *Secrets of Self Mastery*. Twitter: @MitchHorowitz | Instagram: @MitchHorowitz23

CPSIA information can be obtained
at www.ICGtesting.com
Printed in the USA
LVHW052058310121
677957LV00036B/2156